The little boy who changed the world

By V.E. WOODS

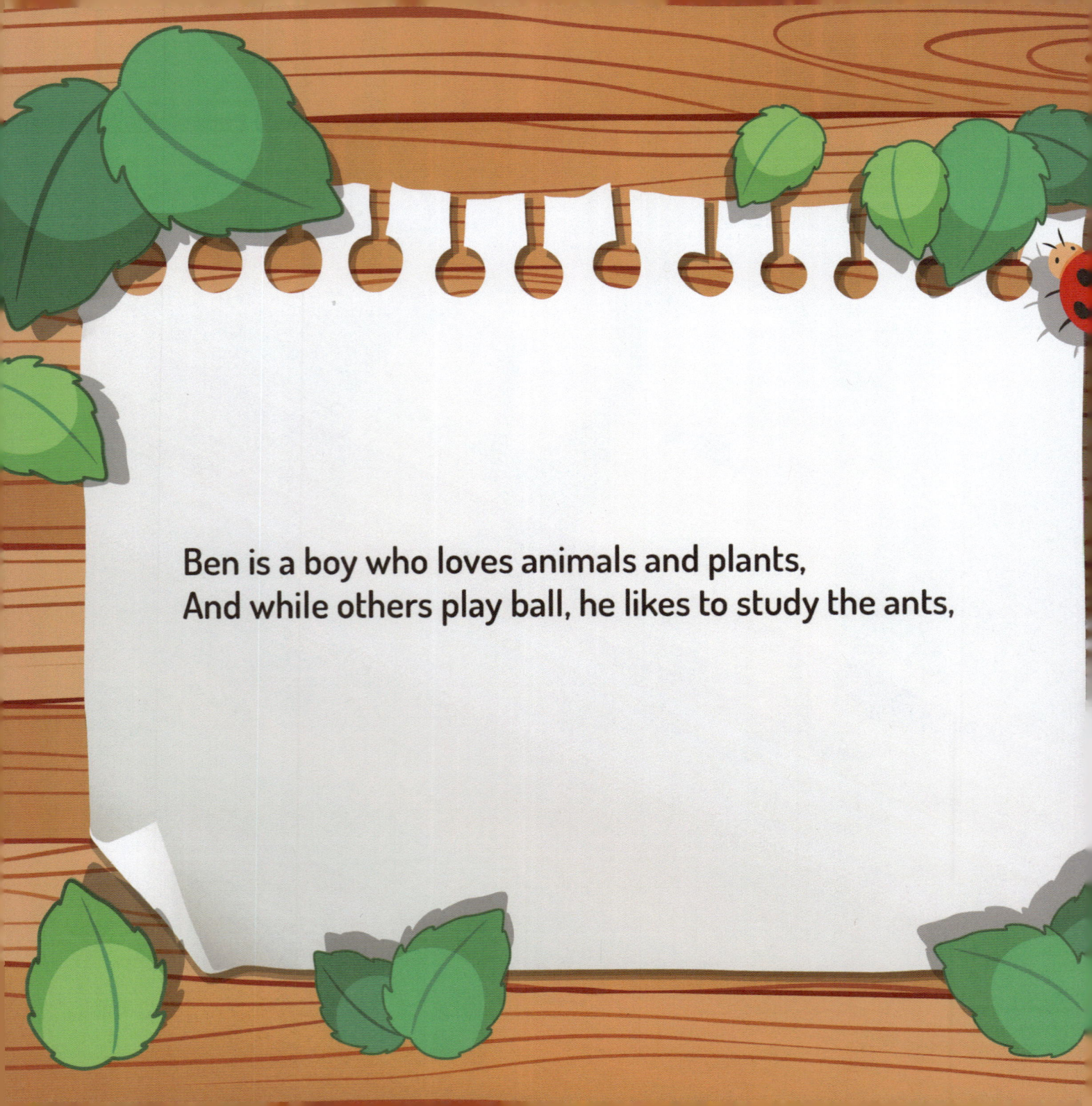

Ben is a boy who loves animals and plants,
And while others play ball, he likes to study the ants,

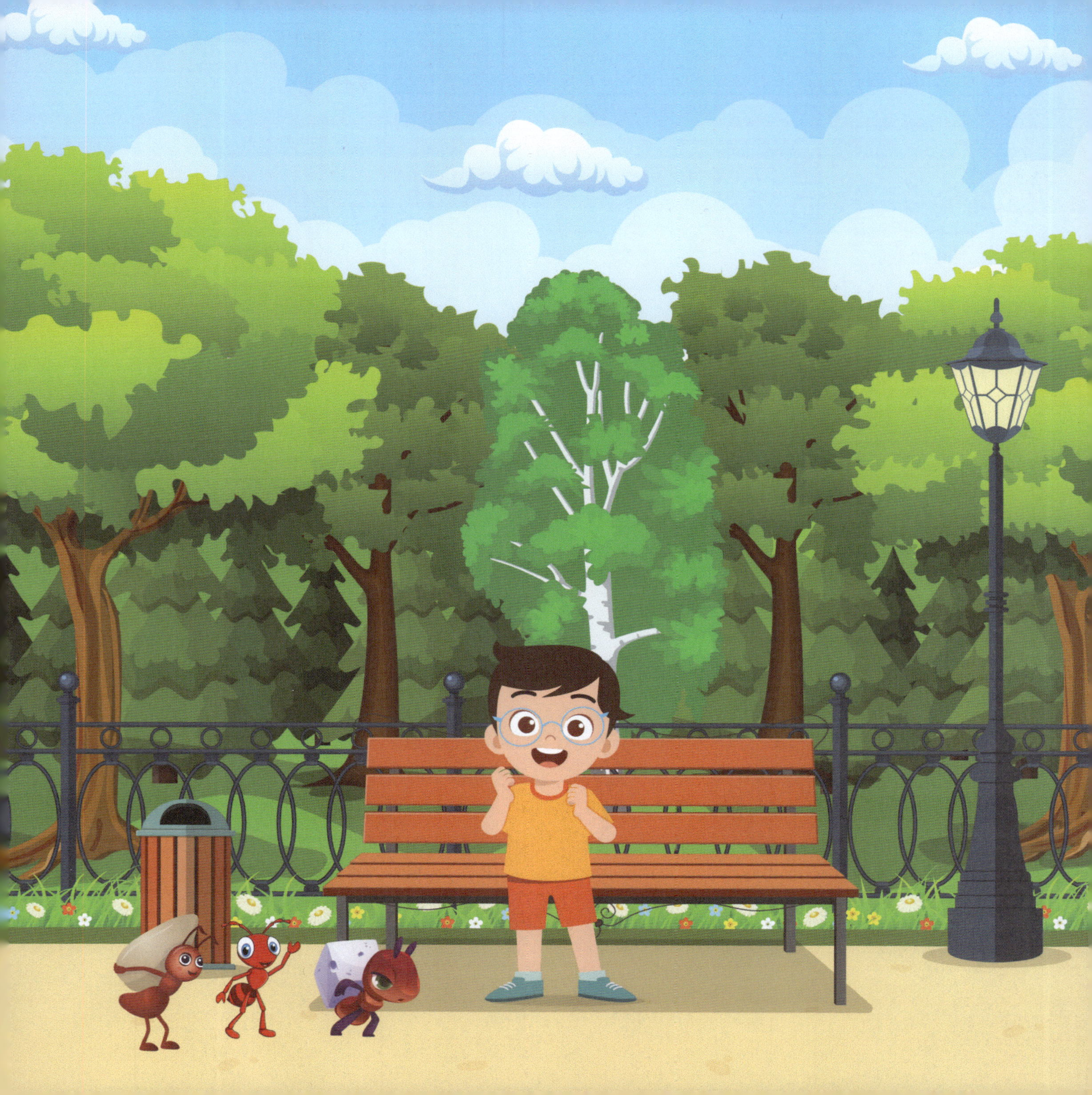

He loves to watch as they scurry to and fro,
What do they carry and where do they go?

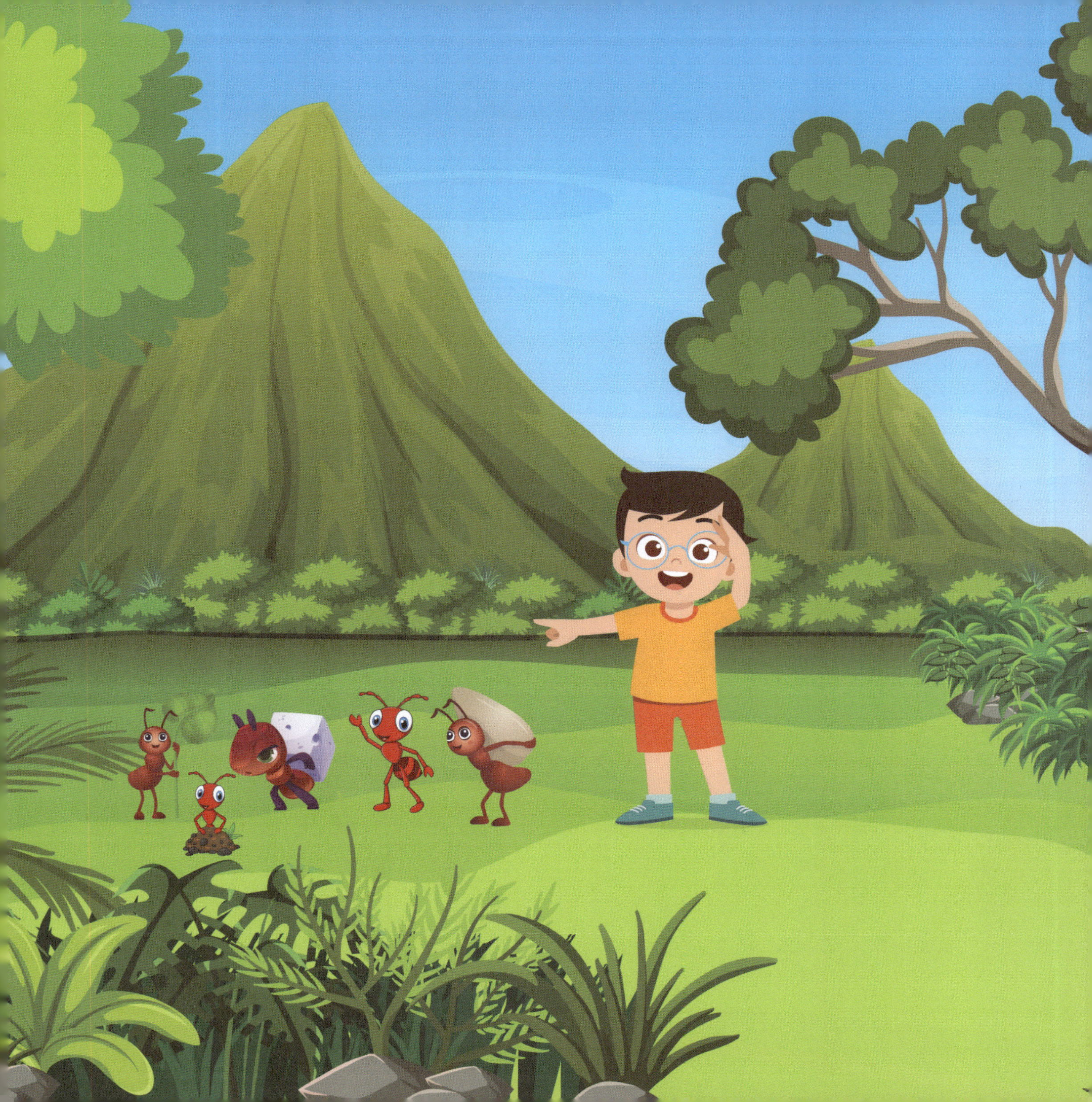

Next, Ben watches the foxes as they play by their den,
Chasing and barking, before scampering home again.

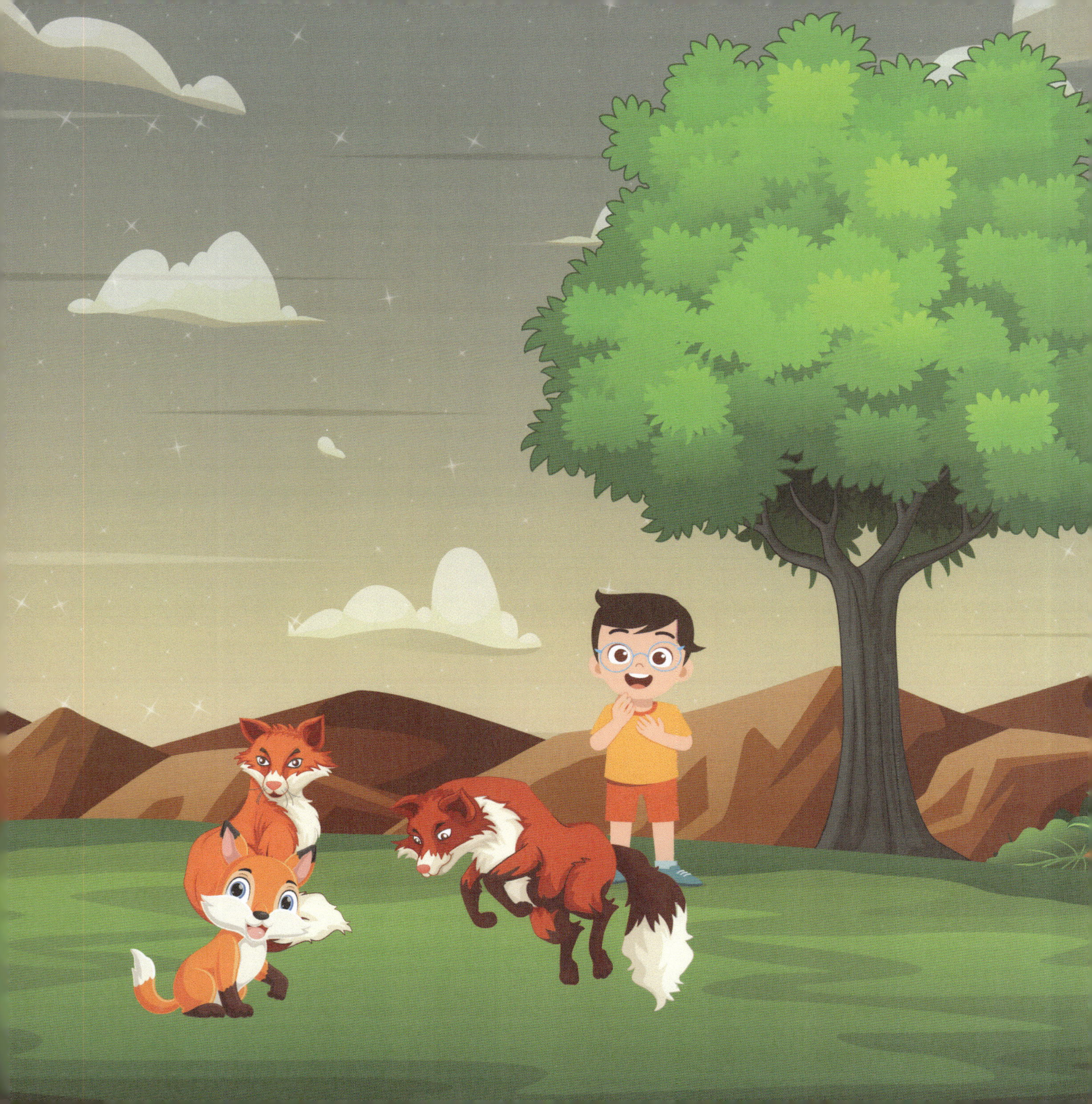

Ben also loves to learn about shrubs and trees,
Woodlands, grasslands, the rivers and seas.

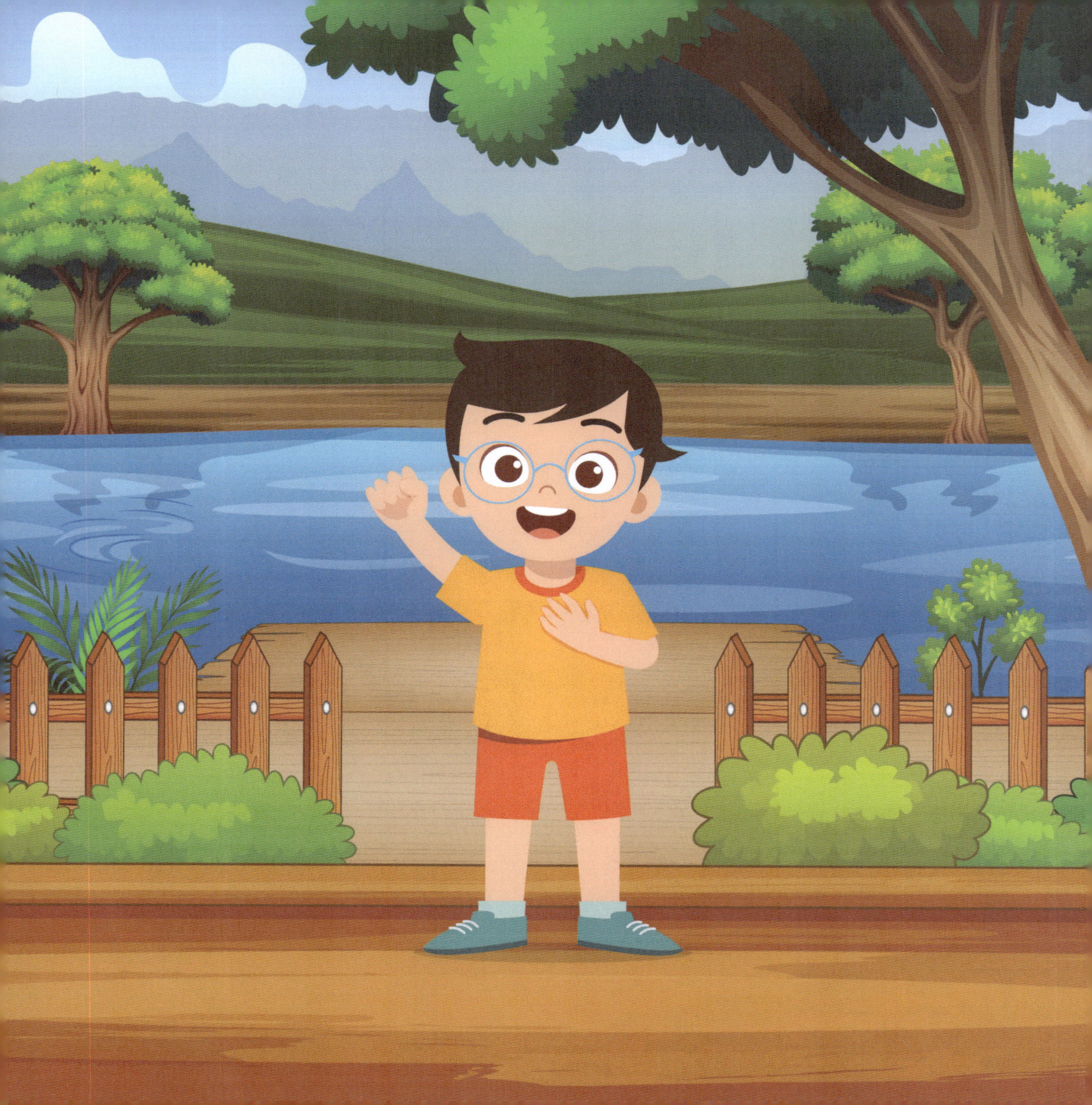

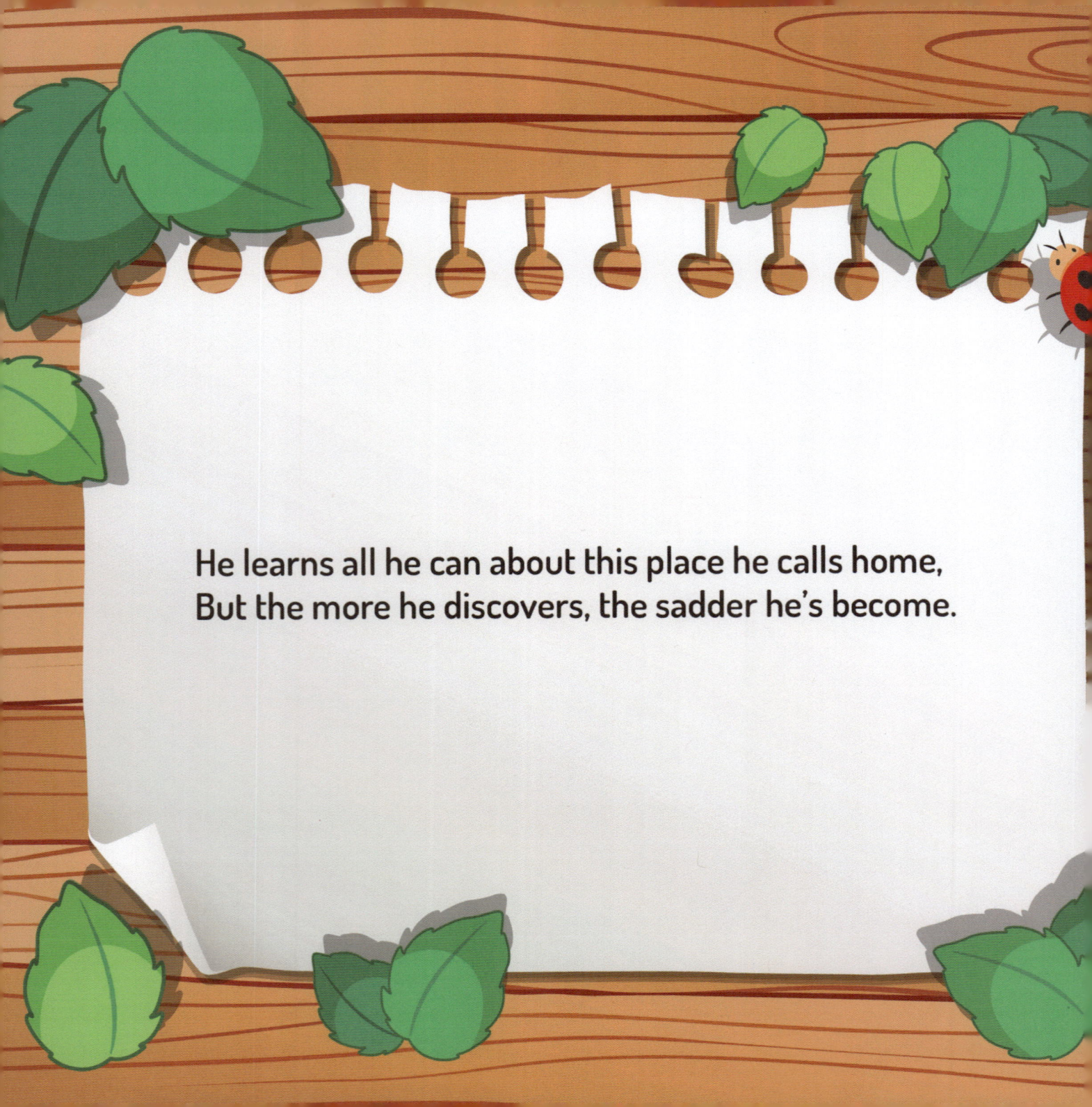

He learns all he can about this place he calls home,
But the more he discovers, the sadder he's become.

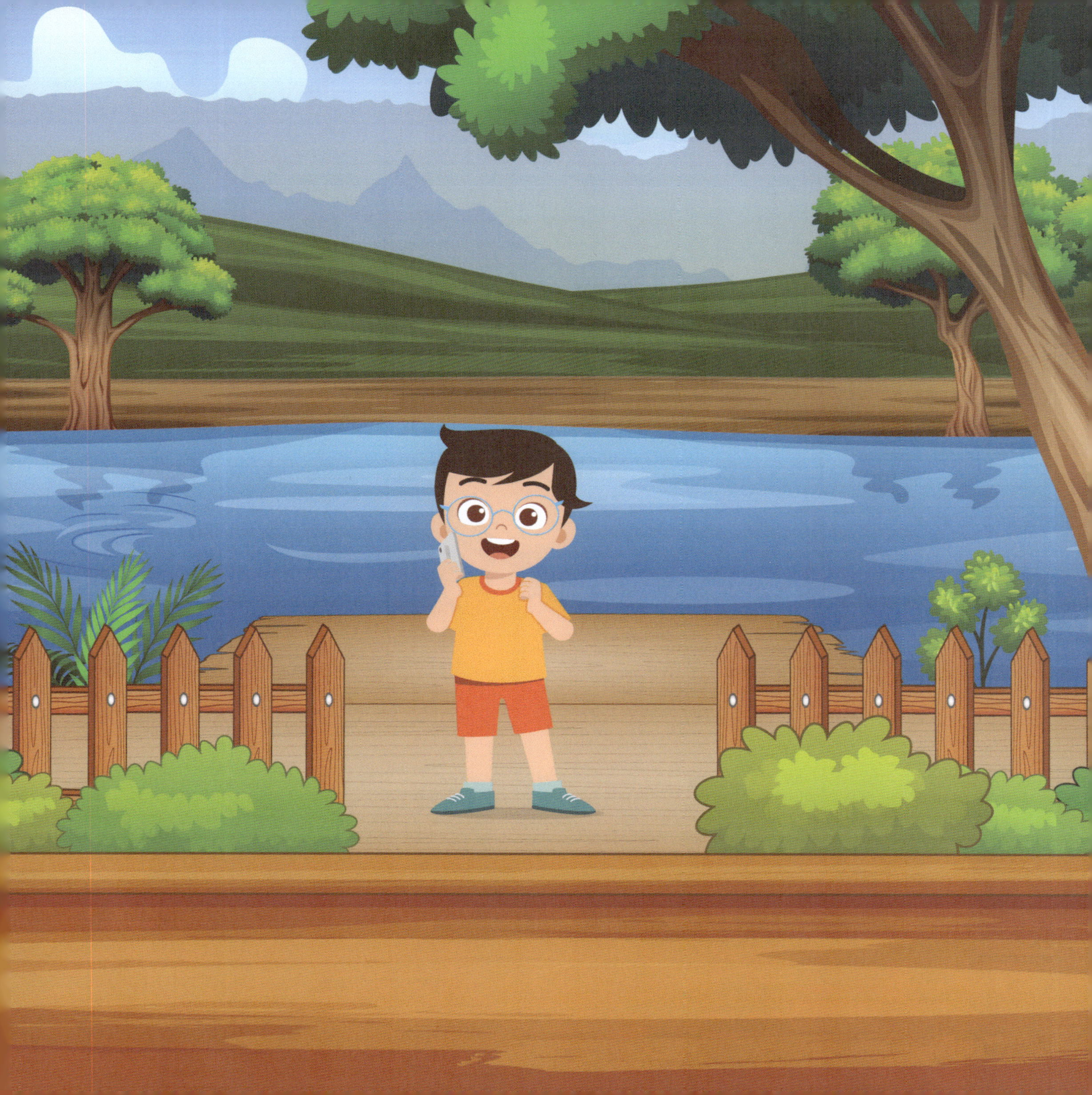

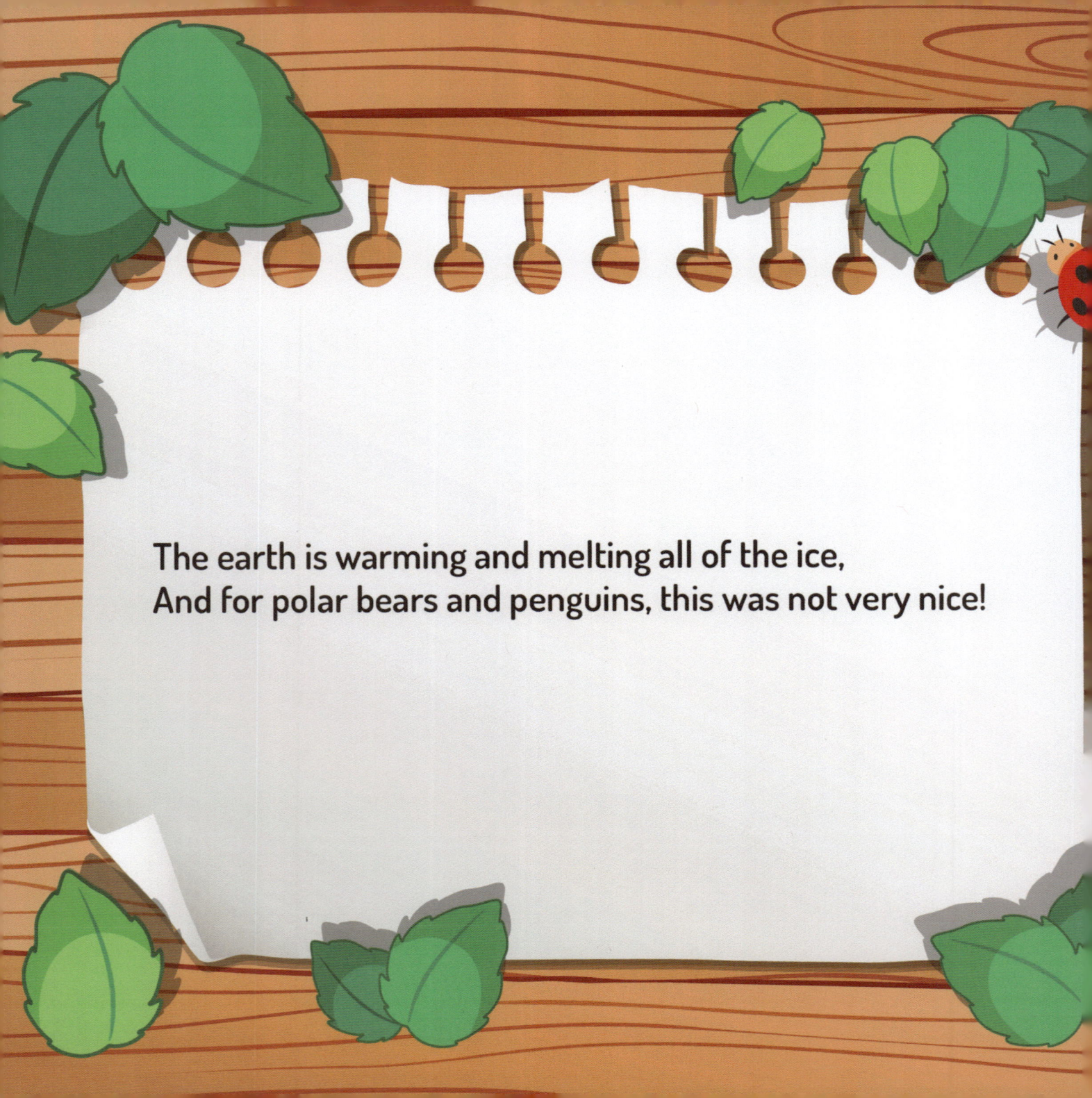

The earth is warming and melting all of the ice,
And for polar bears and penguins, this was not very nice!

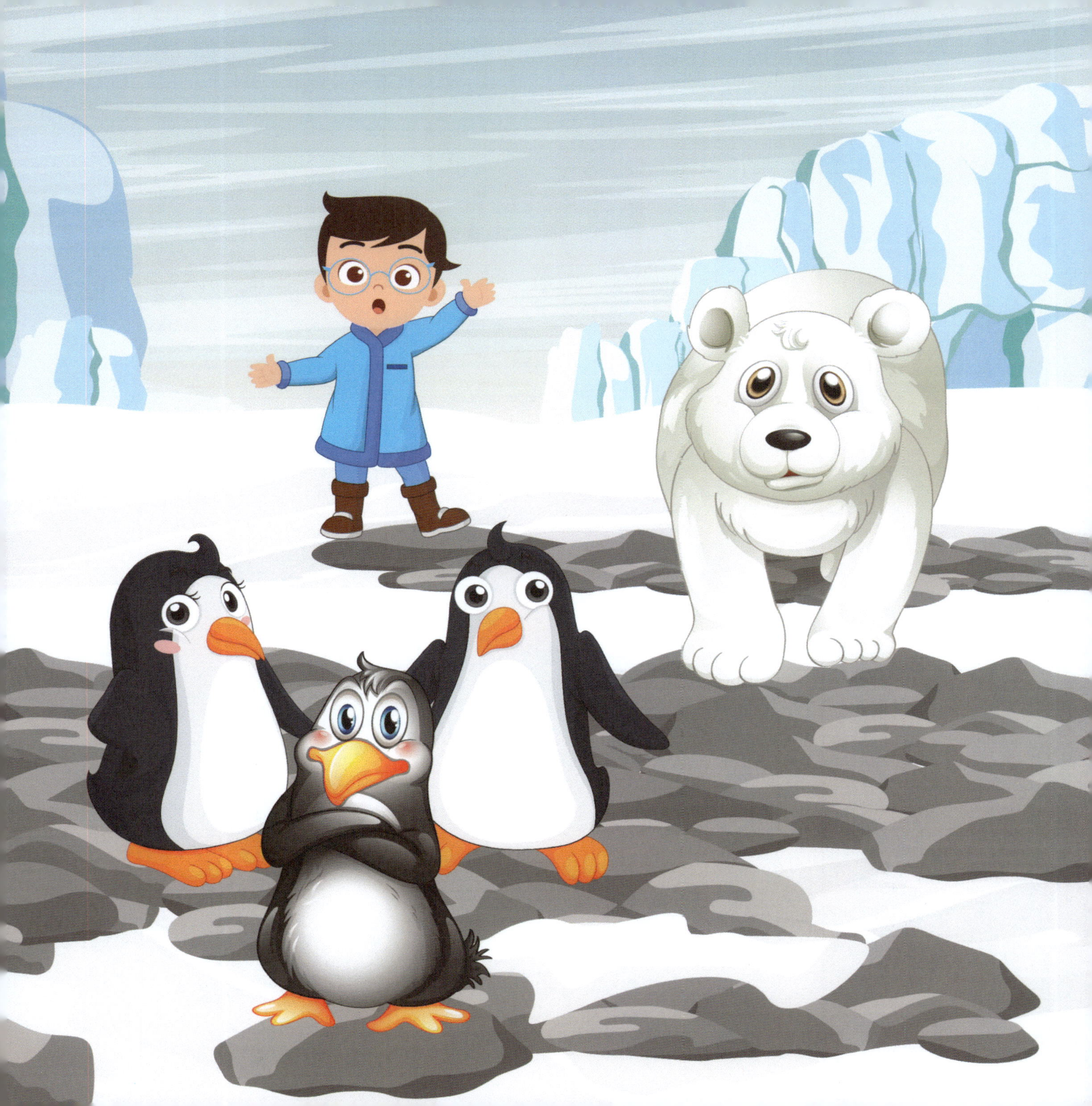

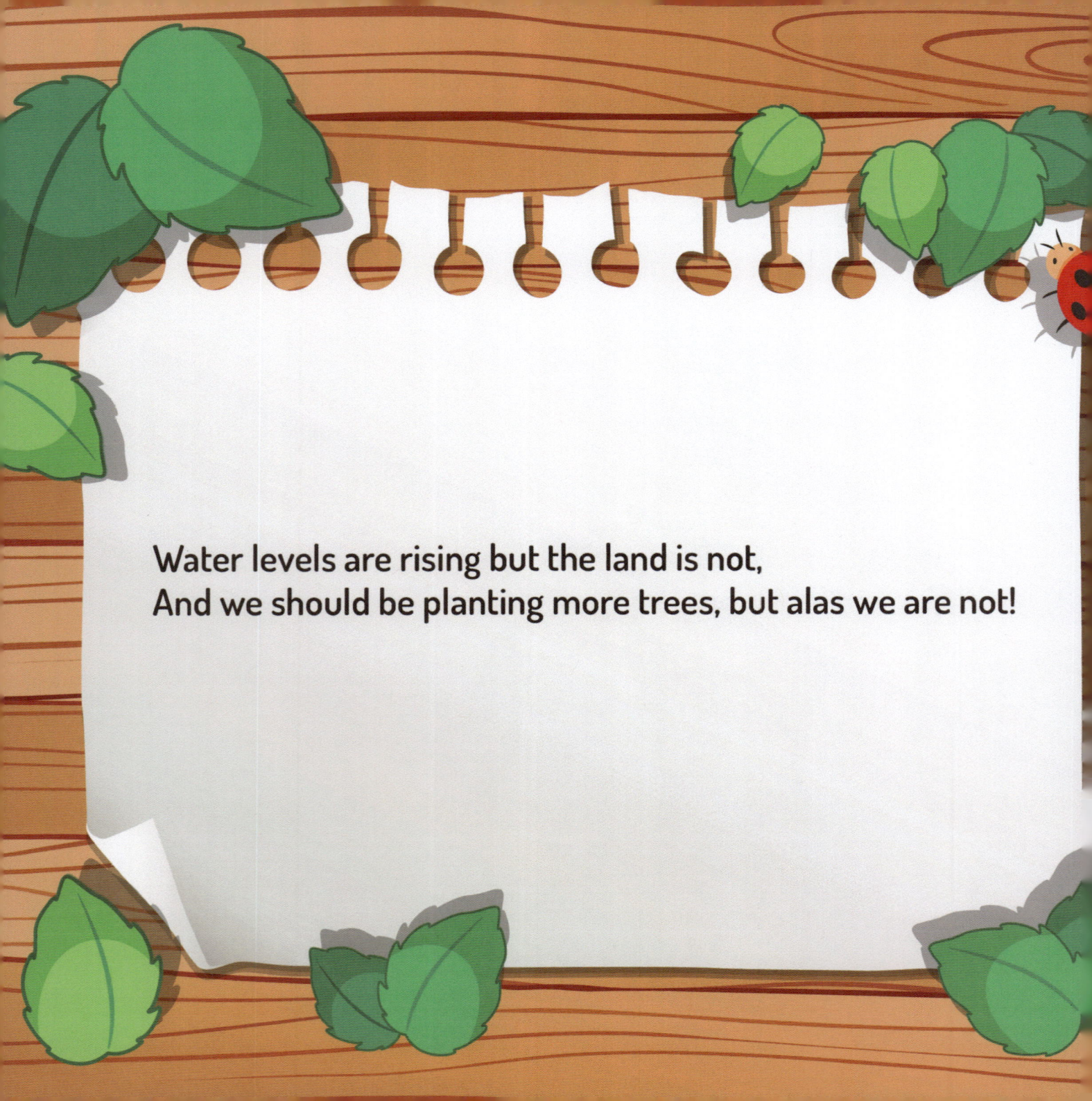

Water levels are rising but the land is not,
And we should be planting more trees, but alas we are not!

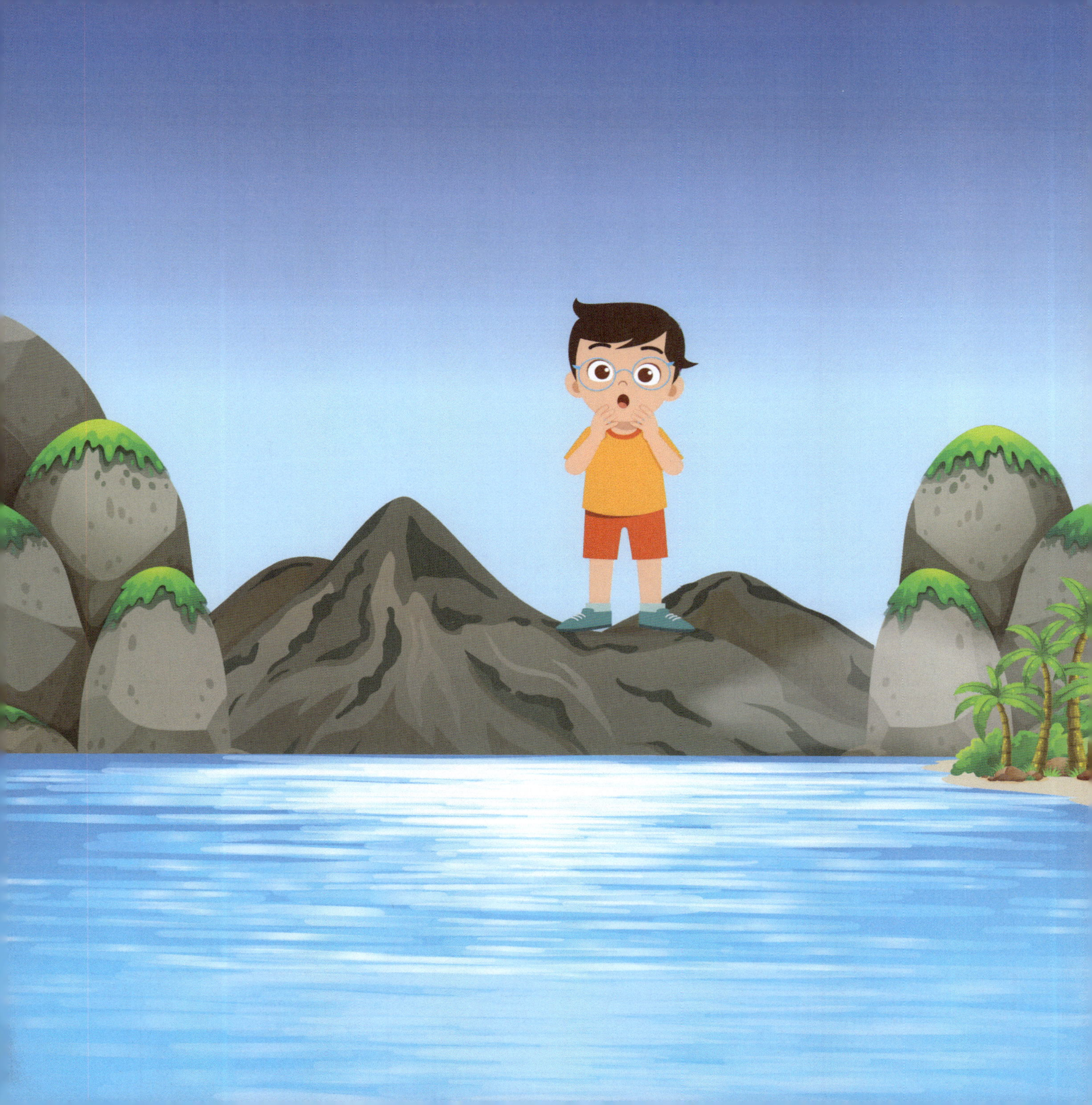

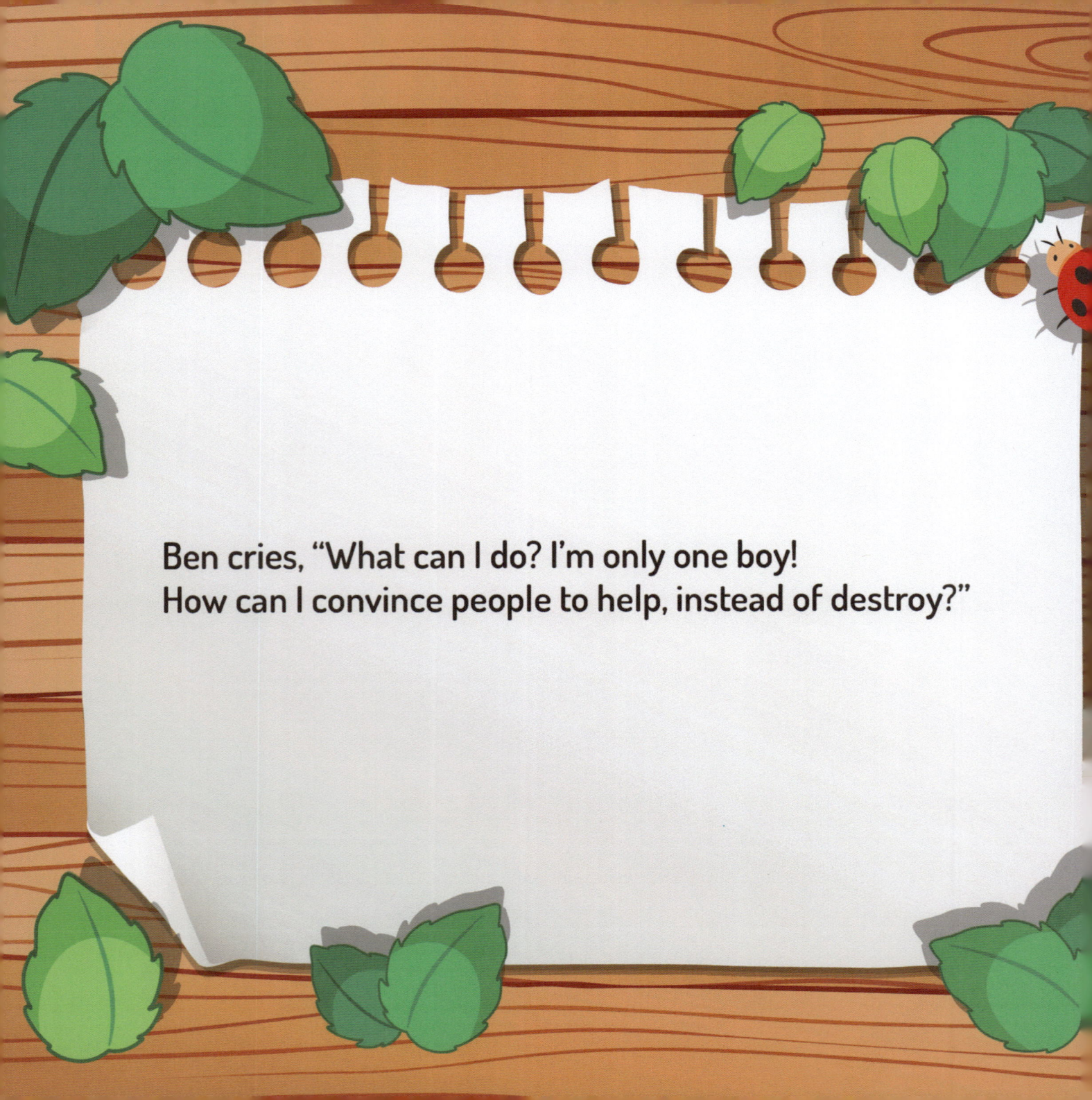

Ben cries, "What can I do? I'm only one boy! How can I convince people to help, instead of destroy?"

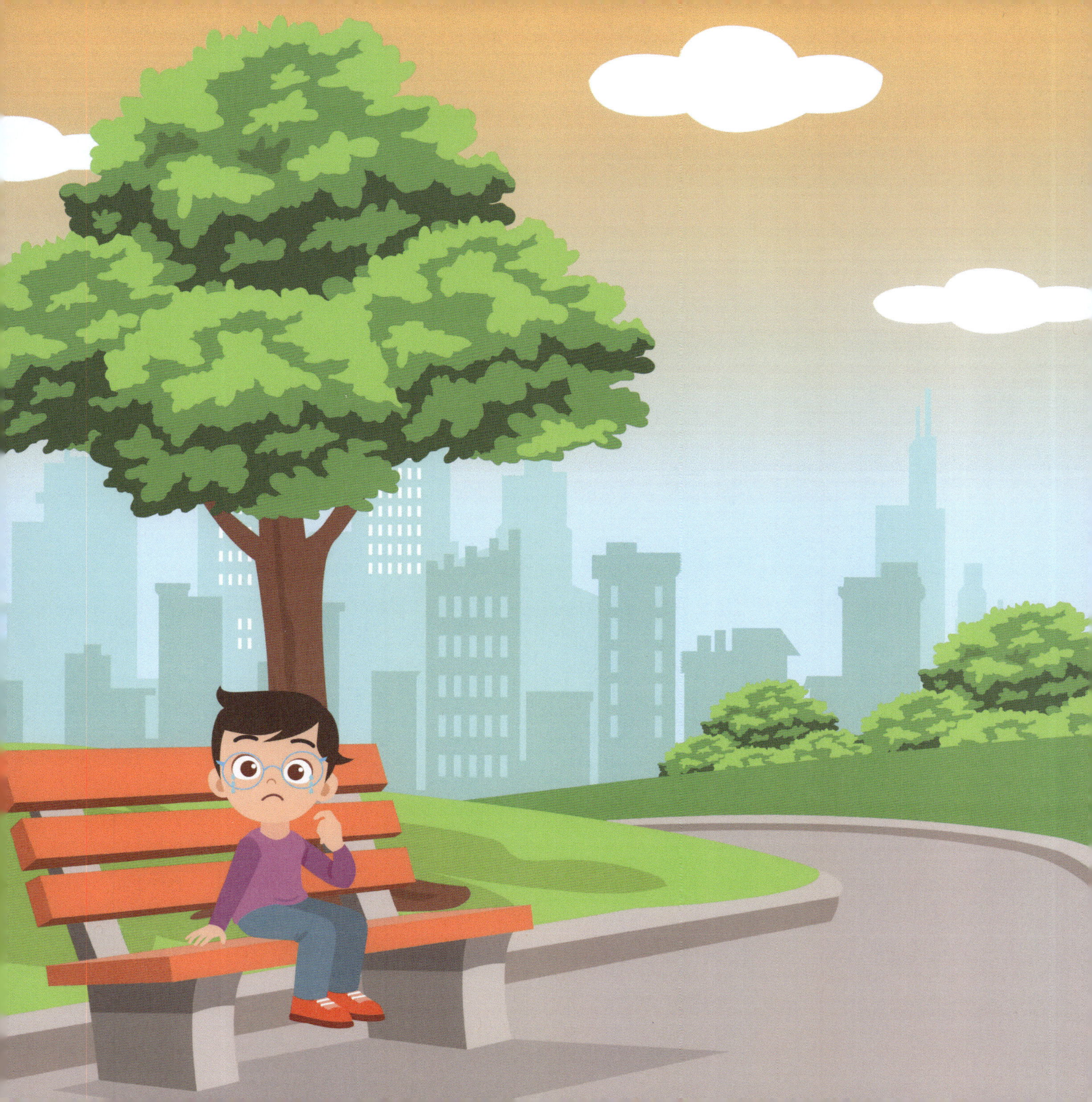

I'll start very small and plant just one tree,
But before very long, Ben had planted three.

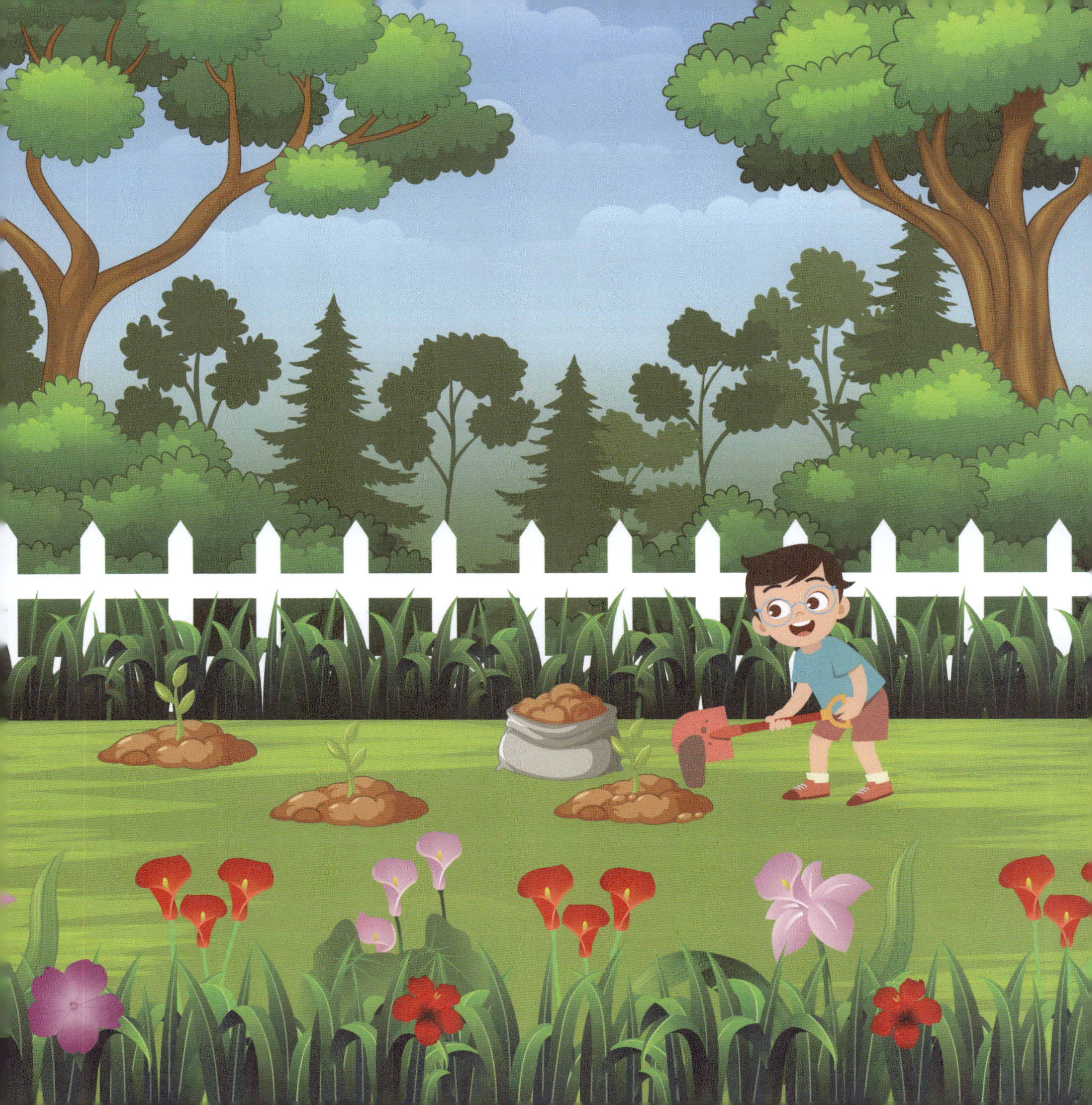

He tells his friends, and soon word spreads,
"What a wonderful idea! We'll all help!" they said.

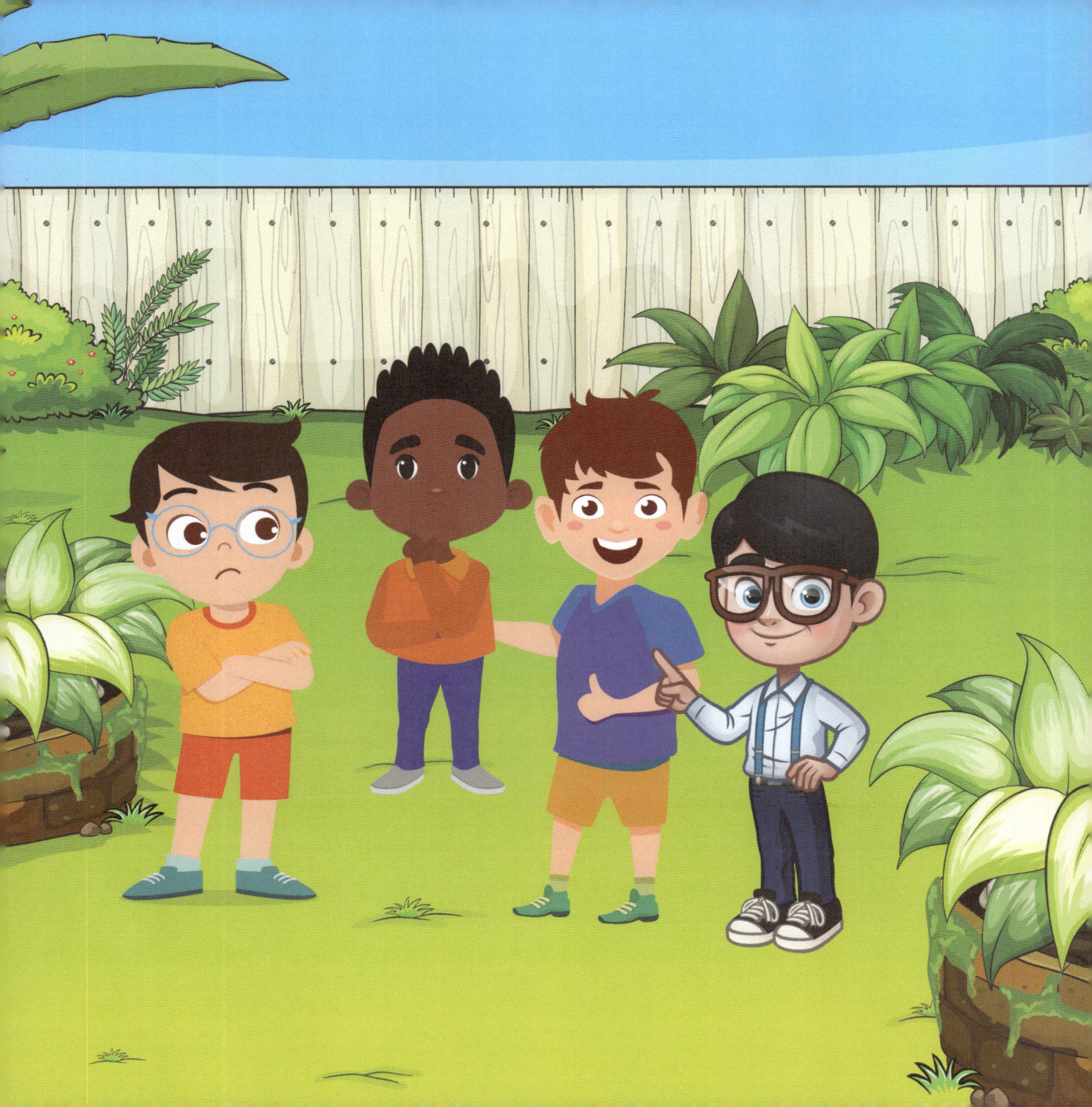

So, they did one beach clean-up... then another few,
Gathering lots of plastic and recycling it all too.

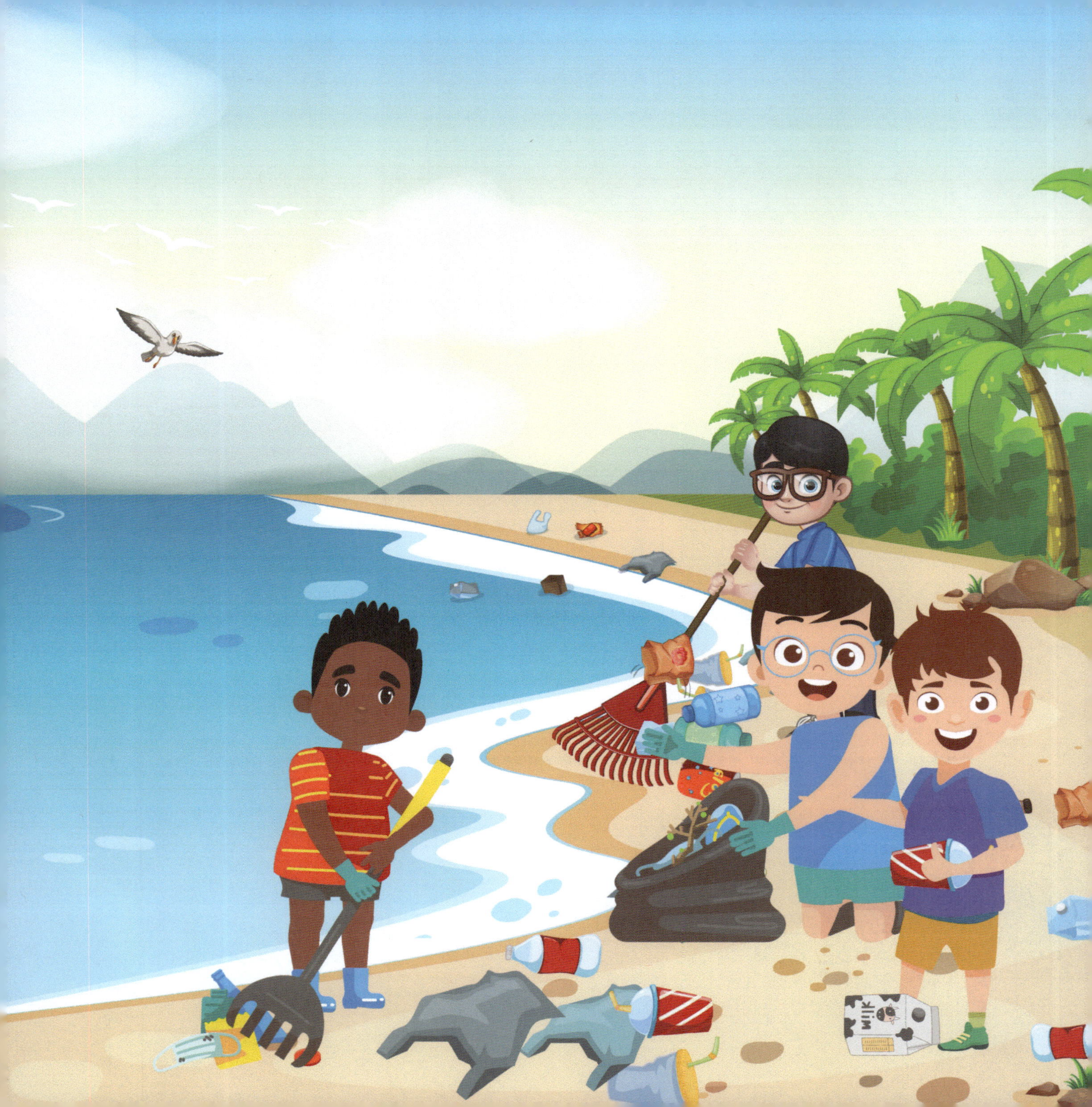

The kind acts soon spread to towns everywhere,
As people learn more about the planet and the home that we share.

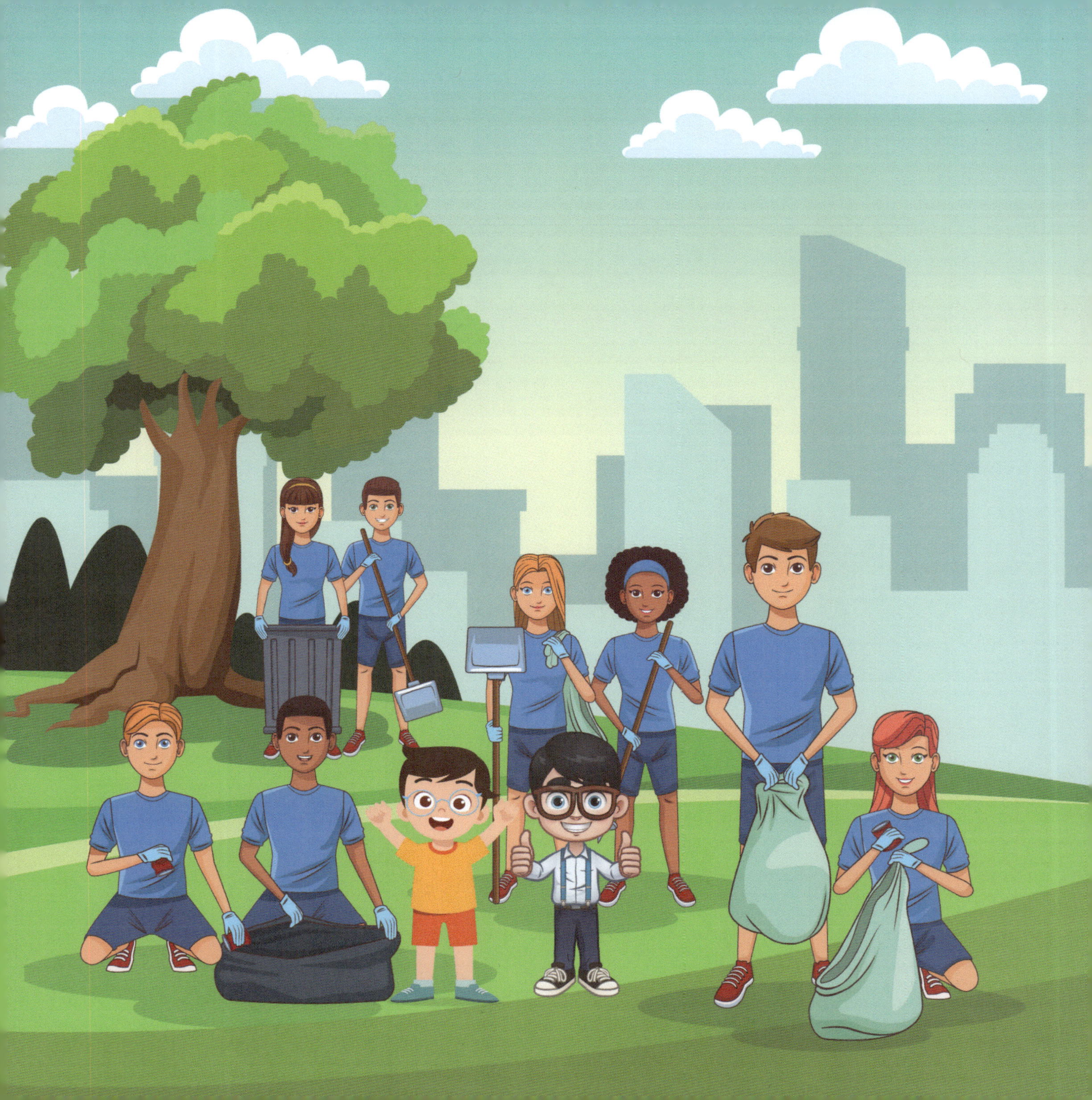

They planted trees, and wildflower meadows too,
They travelled on bikes, enjoying the view.

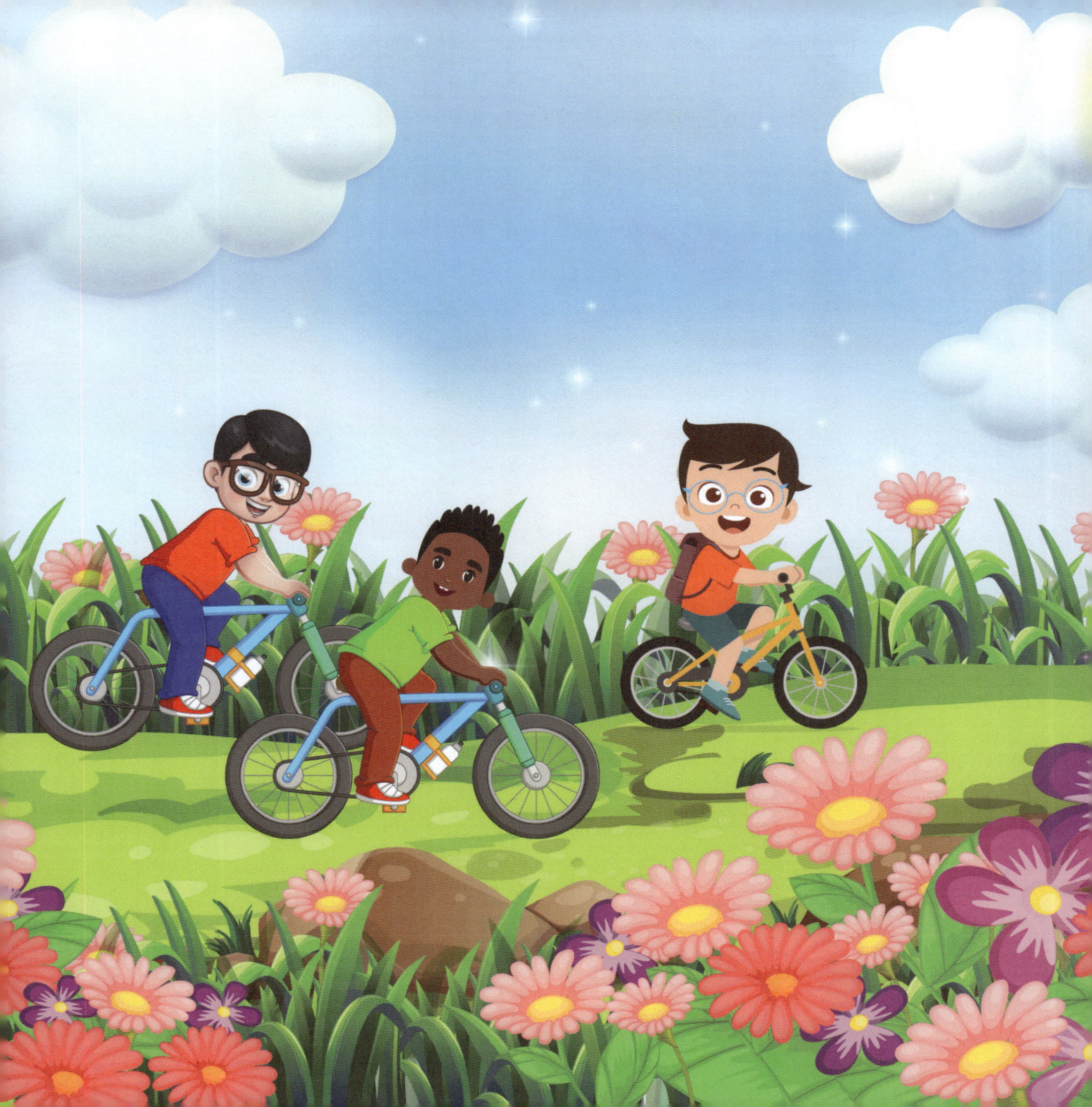

And little by little, the earth began to change,
The seas grew cleaner and where once it was dry, now there was rain.

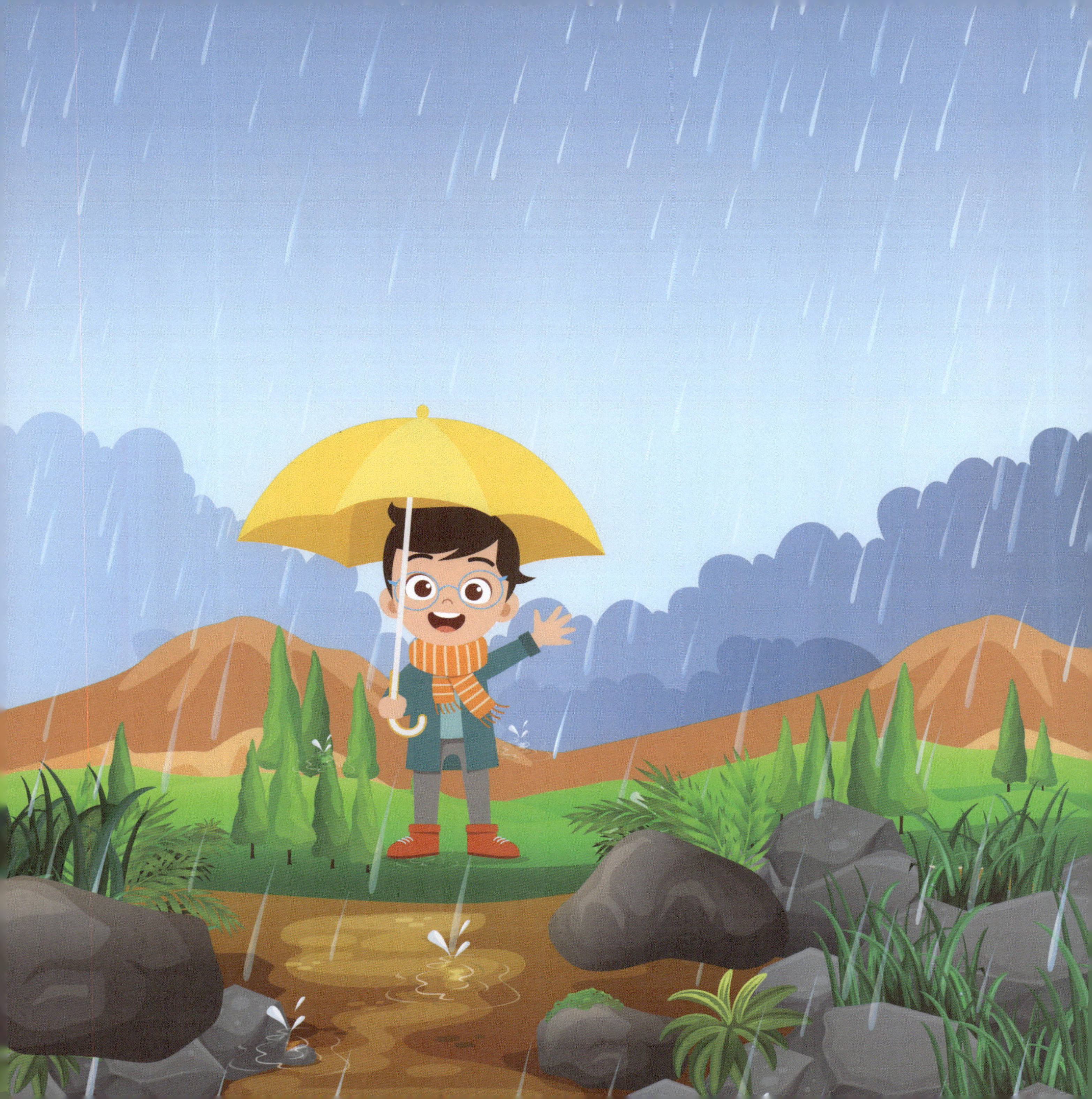

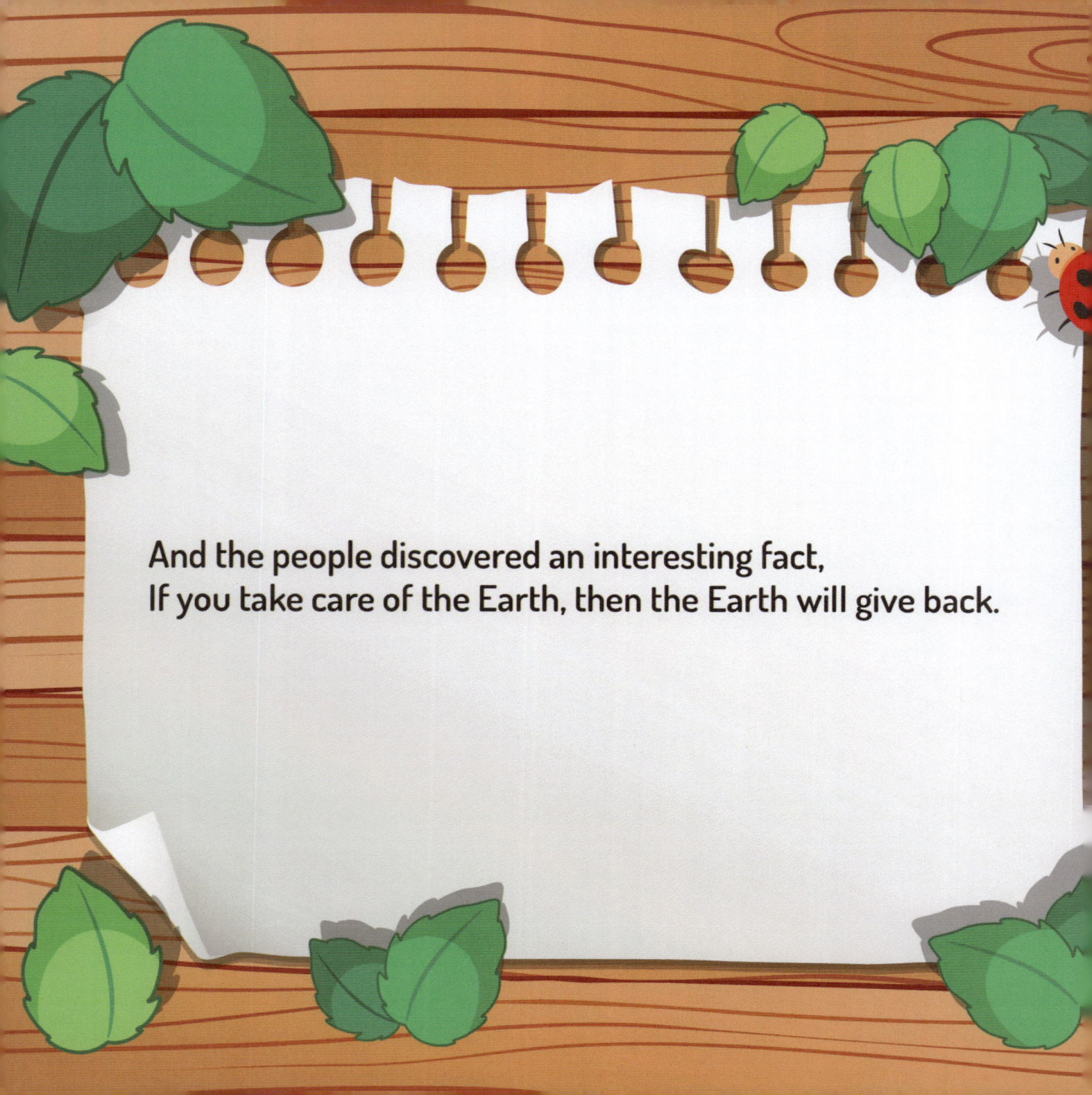

And the people discovered an interesting fact,
If you take care of the Earth, then the Earth will give back.

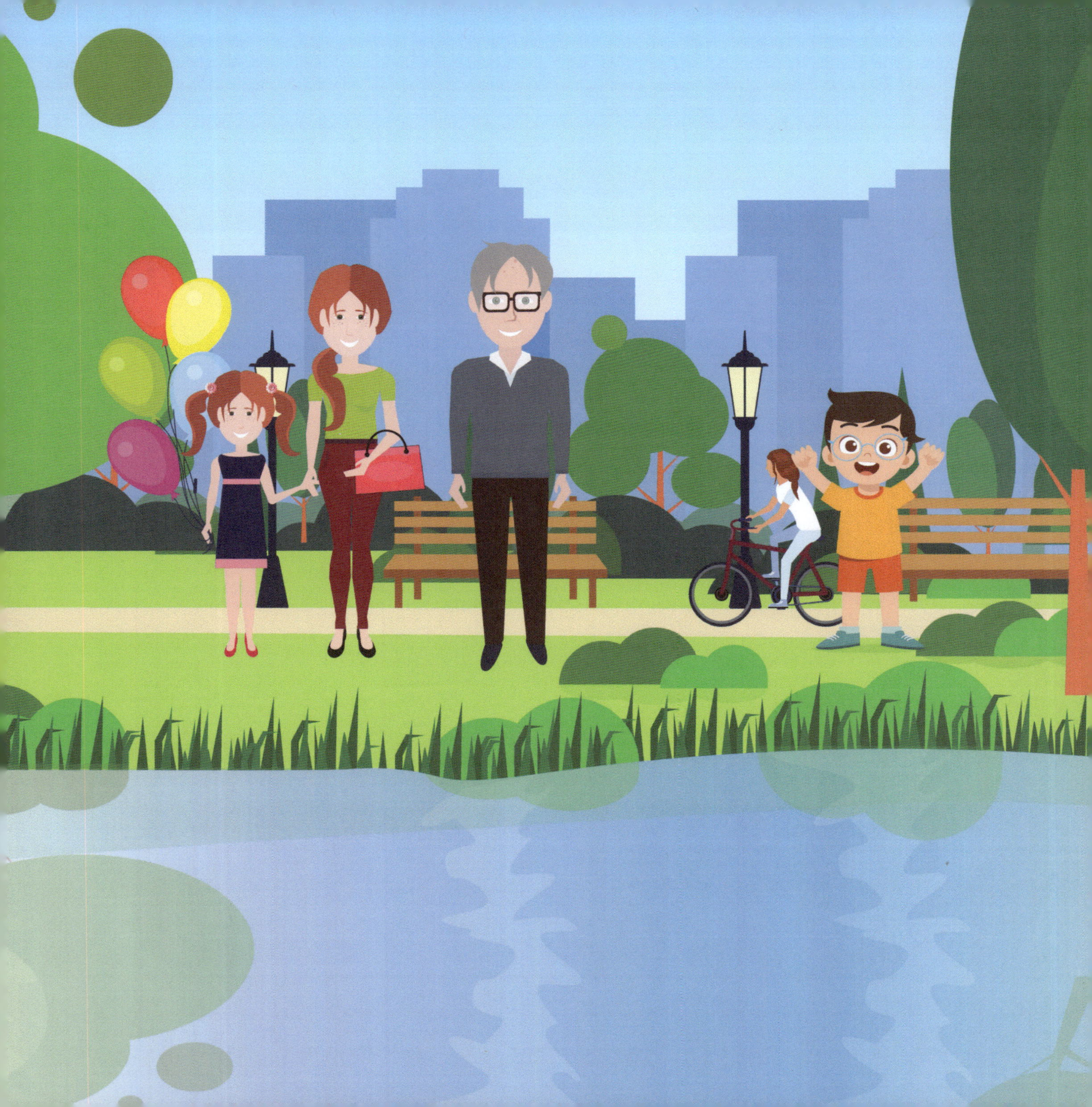

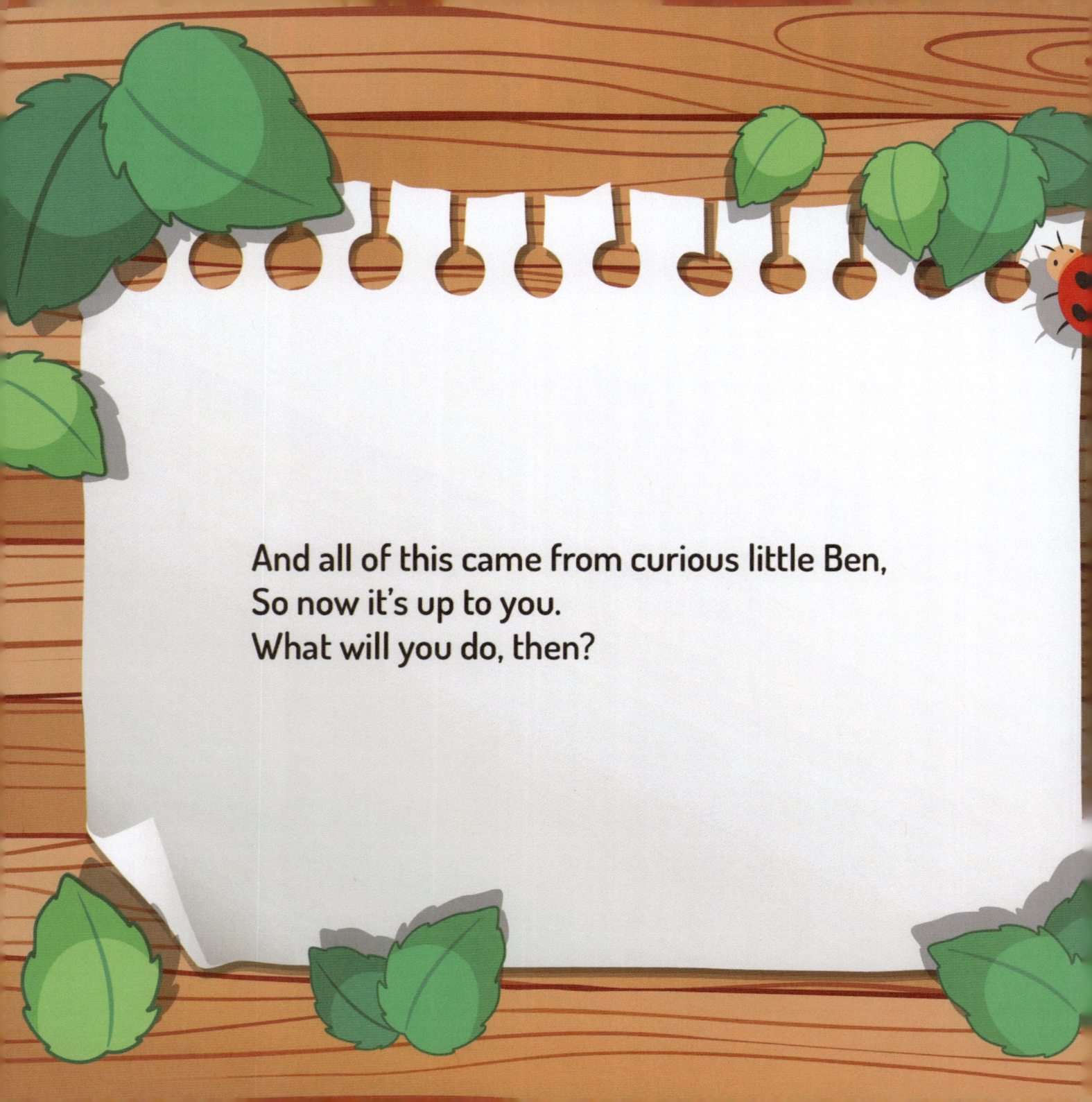

And all of this came from curious little Ben,
So now it's up to you.
What will you do, then?

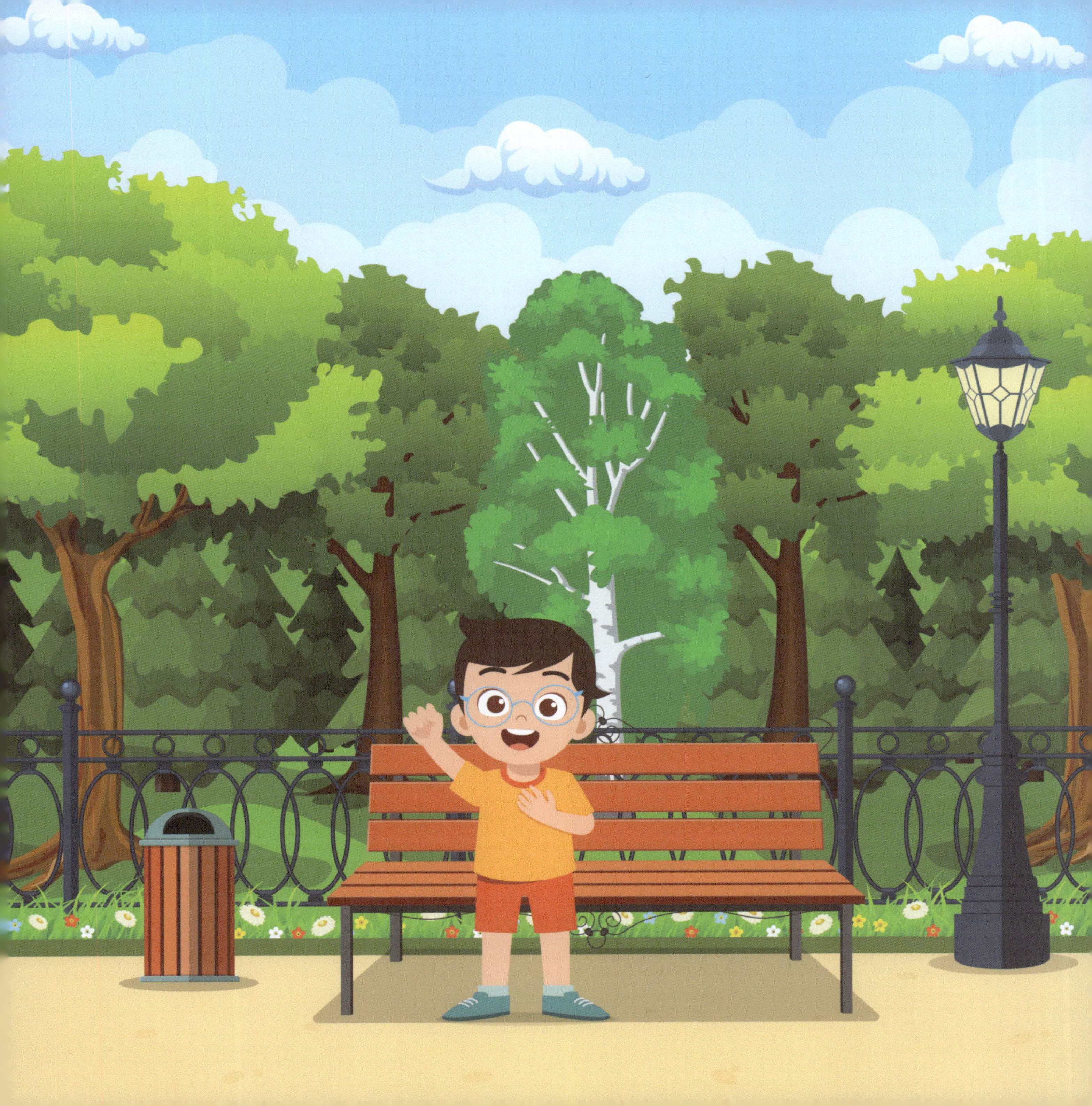

For my brother, working to protect this world.
For my son, who has changed mine.

Printed in Great Britain
by Amazon